SPIDER-MAN™

The Movie Storybook

HarperCollins*Entertainment*

An Imprint of HarperCollins*Publishers*

COLUMBIA PICTURES PRESENTS A MARVEL ENTERPRISES PRODUCTION A LAURA ZISKIN PRODUCTION "SPIDER-MAN"
STARRING: TOBEY MAGUIRE · WILLEM DAFOE · KIRSTEN DUNST · JAMES FRANCO · CLIFF ROBERTSON · ROSEMARY HARRIS
MUSIC BY DANNY ELFMAN   EXECUTIVE PRODUCERS AVI ARAD · STAN LEE   SCREENPLAY BY DAVID KOEPP   BASED ON THE MARVEL COMIC BOOK BY STAN LEE   PRODUCED BY LAURA ZISKIN · IAN BRYCE   DIRECTED BY SAM RAIMI

MARVEL   sony.com/Spider-Man   COLUMBIA
                                                                                            PICTURES

Spider-Man: The Movie Storybook
Spider-Man, the character, ™ & © 2002 Marvel Characters, Inc.
Spider-Man, the movie, © 2002 Columbia Pictures, Industries, Inc.
Photos by Zade Rosenthal: pages 4–11, 13–28, 33, and 36–61
Photos by Steve Kahn: pages 29–32, 34–35, and 63
All rights reserved.

First published in the USA by HarperFestival, a division of HarperCollins*Publishers* in 2002
First published in Great Britain by HarperCollins*Entertainment* in 2002

HarperCollins*Entertainment* is an imprint of
HarperCollins*Publishers* Ltd, 77-85 Fulham Palace Road,
Hammersmith, London W6 8JB

The HarperCollins website address is
www.**fire**and**water**.com

1 3 5 7 9 8 6 4 2
ISBN 0 00 713796 6

Printed and bound in Great Britain by Scotprint

GO FOR THE ULTIMATE SPIN AT:
www.sony.com/Spider-Man

SPIDER-MAN™

The Movie Storybook

Adapted by Shane Coll

Based on the screenplay by David Koepp

Photography by Zade Rosenthal and Steve Kahn

HarperCollins*Entertainment*
An Imprint of HarperCollinsPublishers

 # **Chapter One:**
Poor Peter Parker

Peter Parker was an ordinary teenager. But that was about to change. . . .

Peter lived with his aunt May and uncle Ben. And right next door lived the most popular and interesting girl in his class, Mary Jane Watson.

One day, Mary Jane and Peter's class
went on a field trip to a science laboratory.
The guide told them all about spiders—their
amazing strength and speed, and their
unique ability to spin webs.

The scientists had been doing different experiments, trying to create a new kind of spider.

While Peter was taking photos for the school newspaper, one of the laboratory spiders bit Peter.

"Ow!" he cried.

Peter's life would never be the same.

The next morning, Peter woke up feeling
stronger than he had ever felt before.
He no longer needed his glasses.

He was amazingly agile. He could run super-fast. He developed a strange sense that warned him of danger.

He could shoot webbing from his wrists.

Peter could cling to walls. He had all the abilities of spiders!

Peter wondered what he could do with his spider powers. When he saw Mary Jane drive off with a guy in a flashy new car, Peter had an idea.

He could use his powers to make money to buy a car. Maybe then Peter would be popular, too.

Peter read an ad for a wrestling contest. With his new strength, he could win the cash prize.

Peter told his uncle he was going to the library. Uncle Ben insisted on driving him downtown. Uncle Ben wanted to talk to Peter. "You're changing," Uncle Ben told him. "When I was your age I went through the same thing."

"Not exactly," said Peter. *If his uncle only knew!*

"These are the years when a man becomes the man he's going to be for the rest of his life. Just be careful who you change into," said Uncle Ben. "You're feeling this great power, and with great power comes great responsibility."

Peter was barely listening. He hurried out of the car and over to the wrestling ring.

Peter changed into a costume he had made and went into the caged ring.

The wrestler was strong and fast—but no match for Peter's spider-powers. Peter quickly defeated him. But the manager wouldn't give Peter the money he had promised.

17

"A hundred bucks?" protested Peter. "The ad said three thousand!"

But the manager would not pay the full amount. "I missed the part where that's my problem," he said with a sneer.

Moments later, a thief stole all of the money from the wrestling manager.

Peter could have easily stopped the thief, but instead, he let him run away.

"You just let him go!" a security guard said.

"I missed the part where that's my problem," said Peter. He sounded just like the crooked manager.

Unfortunately, that thief did become Peter's problem.

The thief stole a car to get away from the wrestling ring. He killed the driver of that car—Ben Parker.

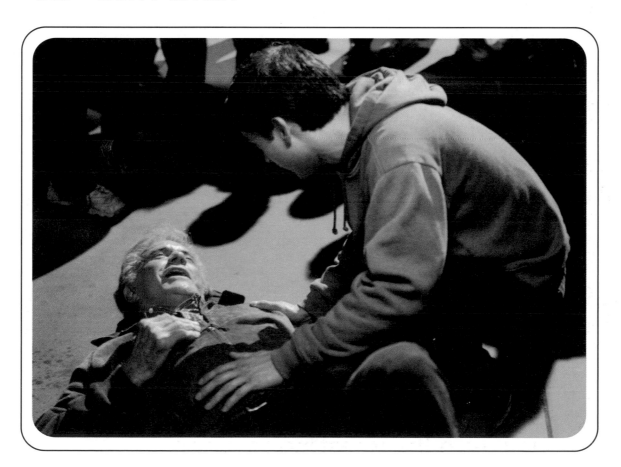

Chapter Two:
Spider-Man to the Rescue

That spring, Peter graduated from high school. He and Aunt May both wished Uncle Ben could have been there.

Peter could not change the past, but he could take responsibility for the future.

He had a new idea about how to use his spider-powers, and it had nothing to do with money or fame.

Peter moved to the city with his friend Harry Osborn.

Harry was the son of a powerful weapons builder named Norman Osborn.

Mr. Osborn was experimenting with a process that would turn average people into soldiers with superhuman strength. "We are unlocking the secrets of human evolution," he announced.

The army did not want to wait any longer for results. The generals were going to cancel their funding if OsCorp did not provide a successful test of their experiments.

Mr. Osborn decided it was time for a human trial. And he would be the test subject.

Deep in the OsCorp building, Mr. Osborn strapped himself into a glass tank. A thick gas filled the tank.

Something went terribly wrong.

Meanwhile, Peter was trying to balance his life as a student with his new identity as Spider-Man!

Spider-Man swung, swooped, and soared among the tall buildings.

He captured criminals.

He rescued innocent people.

He foiled bank robbers.

He protected the city.

Spider-Man became famous. Peter set a camera into some webbing on a wall and took pictures of himself in costume. He was able to sell the photos to a newspaper.

"Bring me more shots of that newspaper-selling clown!" shouted the editor, J. J. Jameson. A headline read: SPIDER-MAN, HERO OR MENACE?

Peter did not like what the paper wrote about Spider-Man, but he needed the money.

Peter was enjoying his adventures as Spider-Man, but his favorite times were when he met with Mary Jane. She had moved to the city to become an actress.

Right now, she was working as a waitress, but he knew she would be a star. Right now, she was dating Harry, but Peter hoped that would change, too.

Chapter Three:
Beware the Green Goblin

Peter was photographing scenes from the World Unity Day celebration, when a costumed figure arrived. It was the Green Goblin! He swooped down over the crowd on his glider.

Then the Green Goblin went on the attack!
The police could not hold him back. He went
after the men who controlled OsCorp—and
Harry and Mary Jane were with them.

Spider-Man rushed to the scene. He battled the Green Goblin on the ground and high above the buildings. Spider-Man shot webbing into the Green Goblin's face. The Green Goblin took off, clawing away at the webbing in his eyes.

Spider-Man rescued Mary Jane from a
crumbling ledge. He left her safely in a
rooftop garden.

"But wait, who are you?" she called after him.

"Just your friendly neighborhood Spider-Man," he answered.

Then he leaped back into the sky.

The next day, the Green Goblin was back. He attacked the *Daily Bugle* office.

"Who's the photographer who takes pictures of Spider-Man?" he demanded. "I need to talk to him about his favorite subject."

Luckily, Peter was dropping off photos. He
changed into his Spider-Man costume. The
Green Goblin sprayed knock-out gas at
Spider-Man and took him to a tall rooftop.

"Imagine what we could accomplish together," offered the Green Goblin. He wanted Spider-Man for a partner! "Think about it, hero."

But Peter didn't have to. He was dedicated to protecting the city.

Peter hurried home for Thanksgiving dinner. Aunt May was cooking for him, Mr. Osborn, Harry, and Mary Jane.

As the group was sitting down to eat, Mr. Osborn noticed strange slashes on Peter's arms.

"I stepped off a curb and got clipped by one of those bike messengers," said Peter. He couldn't admit that the Green Goblin had injured him in battle.

Mr. Osborn left the dinner abruptly. "I'm afraid I have to go," he said. "Something . . . has come to my attention."

Later that night, the Green Goblin attacked again. This time his victim was Aunt May!

The villain knew that Spider-Man was really Peter Parker. And he knew who Peter cared about most.

Peter hurried to the hospital. Luckily, Aunt May would recover.

Then Peter thought: What if the Green Goblin knew about the other person he cared for?

Peter ran to the phone to call Mary Jane.
He heard a horrible cackling over the line.
"Can Spider-Man come out and play?"
asked a voice. The Green Goblin had
captured Mary Jane!

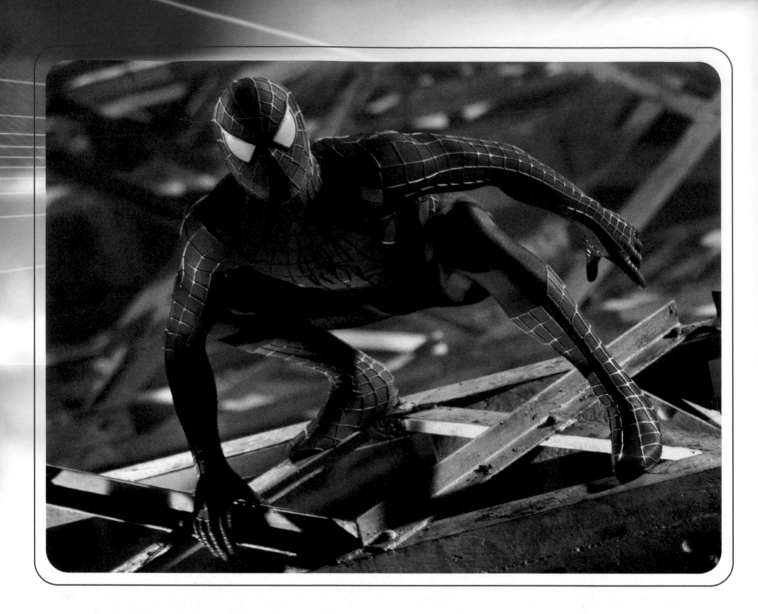

The Green Goblin held Mary Jane atop a high bridge. He also held on to a cable—the lone support of a dangling tram. He gave Spider-Man a choice: Save Mary Jane or save the tram full of innocent children. "Choose!" screamed the Green Goblin. He released the cable at the same time that he pushed Mary Jane into the air.

Spider-Man leapt off the bridge and grabbed Mary Jane in midair. At the same time he shot a web around the tram. He held the cable in one hand and Mary Jane in the other. The children and Mary Jane were saved!

But the battle with the Green Goblin was
just beginning. He launched a line at Spider-
Man's waist, yanking the hero after him
on his glider. Spider-Man crashed into an
abandoned building.

The Green Goblin swooped down and
attacked.

In the fight, the Green Goblin's mask came off. Spider-Man was amazed to find out Mr. Osborn was the Green Goblin. Mr. Osborn's attempts to become a super-soldier had given him enormous strength, but had also driven him insane.

During the brawl, the Green Goblin was killed when his own glider launched at him.

Peter had seen how the Green Goblin had abused his power—and at what cost. More than ever, Peter vowed to live by the words his uncle had said to him: With great power comes great responsibility.